Welc...

Fellow Parents and Guardian Angels,
Thank You For Your Purchase!

Allow me to introduce myself, my name is Orite Levy, owner and curator/designer of,
Assorted Arts Press Kids!.
&
Assorted Arts Press

Not only am I a strong small business owner but a proud single mother of
a growing son and full time caretaker for my 95yo gran & 71yo disabled uncle.
As you can see, family is important to me and so are our children.
It is my goal to make quality books for all.
I would LOVE your feedback.

GIVE ME YOUR THOUGHTS!

!!Bonus!!
**Your reviews matter, If you love this book and leave a
5 star written review, take a screen shot of your submitted review and send it to the email
below, I will send you a free downloadable positive affirmation coloring book! :)**

If you have anything other than a five star review, feel free to leave it if you feel the need
and also, I would ask for your personal feedback.
Please contact me letting me know what YOU would
change to make this book even better.
Let me hear your voices!

Happily raving reviews always welcome...
It takes a community and I am glad to have you as a part of ours.

Direct all comments to Assortedartspress@gmail.com
Include the book you are referencing.
Thanks! :)

Student Information:

Year: ....

Age: ....

Grade: ....

For all of our other books scan the QR code below

SCAN ME

Join our YouTube community!!

"Happy Kids Daily Affirmations!"

SUBSCRIBE

Scan Me!

Videos uploaded regularly, along with many more to choose from for daily affirmation practice...

https://www.youtube.com/@AssortedArtsPressKids/videos

A note to the Adults:

Hello Fellow Adults,

Thank you for choosing this workbook for your growing young minds.
By choosing this book you are setting your children up for success.

Note that the workbook is designed to be simple and repetitive because repetition is how we begin to instill powerful beliefs in ourselves and the simplicity provides a feeling of success and accomplishment. It is also made to be used at different stages of the child's writing experience, once when learning to form smaller letters, once again when they are able to write them on their own freely and then onto sentences.
When your child finishes this workbook they can move on to our Assorted Arts Press Kids! "I AM Positive Affirmation Sentences Handwriting Practice Workbook".
It is my hope and suggestion that you choose to continue this practice of writing positive affirmations with your child far and beyond this early learning experience.
Practice is everything and a strong successful mindset is no different.

When this book is used regularly, or other affirmation practices, you may notice your child walking around talking to themselves in a very different, more uplifting way. This is the beginning of a new way of thinking about themselves and how they take on the situations in their lives. This world can be a very negative place and so can the set of our own minds become quite negative, so why not start the positive mindset training young? Empower your children to overcome life's challenges and rise to the top by feeling confident and worthy, strong enough to reach their goals/dreams.
i know I want that for my son. We may not be able to protect them from the trials and tribulations of life but we CAN give them a powerful mindset to overcome anything with as much grace and ease as is possible. Don't you wish you had had the same?

Another important impression to make is that practice is what gets us to our goals and taking daily action, such as tracing/writing daily will create an outcome, in this case, it is much better penmanship and a high level positive mindset. All cases differ depending on what is being practiced. This style of daily action is setting kids up for successful life habits, for balance and for good mental wellbeing.

Lastly, children learn best by example, so maybe , just maybe, it wouldn't be a bad idea to add I AM Affirmations to your own daily practices. You may find yourself walking around talking to yourself in a very different, more uplifting way. I know I do!

Thank you for your support and for supporting young minds everywhere!

Message to the Kiddos,

(Adult please read to child and translate when needed, make sure the child has a good understanding of this page before beginning the practice.)

Welcome to your positive affirmation practice, this is a practice to be done daily and as much as possible throughout your whole life.

When you do these practices over and over throughout your life, you will build a strong base for all your successes and will be even MORE likely to reach your dreams!

Congratulations to you for making yourself a stronger more successful human being!

Remember this, feeling is everything when saying and learning positive affirmations and for now, one word a day is perfect.

It is important to believe these affirmations with all your heart. To feel as if you actually are what you are affirming because, YOU ARE!

Understand that sometimes in life you will experience people who do not see or understand your dreams and that is o.k. They will likely unintentionally tell you "you can't" and this is just not true.

It may be true for them but only YOU know your own truth!

You have the power to create anything you put your mind, heart and actions toward and it is up to you to disregard the disbelief of others.

Remember not to judge them, they may not realize that they are expressing a limited view and they just can't see beyond their own limits.

You are limitless!!

So, every time you practice in this book make sure you say the affirmation aloud with feelings of joy and empowerment because you are Brilliant, Awesome, Talented and so much more!

You CAN and will succeed at reaching your dreams if you continue to take action toward them everyday in some way and believe first in yourself and not in what others tell you you can or can not accomplish.

You are a shining star, shine baby!

THIS AFFIRMATION WORKBOOK BELONGS TO:

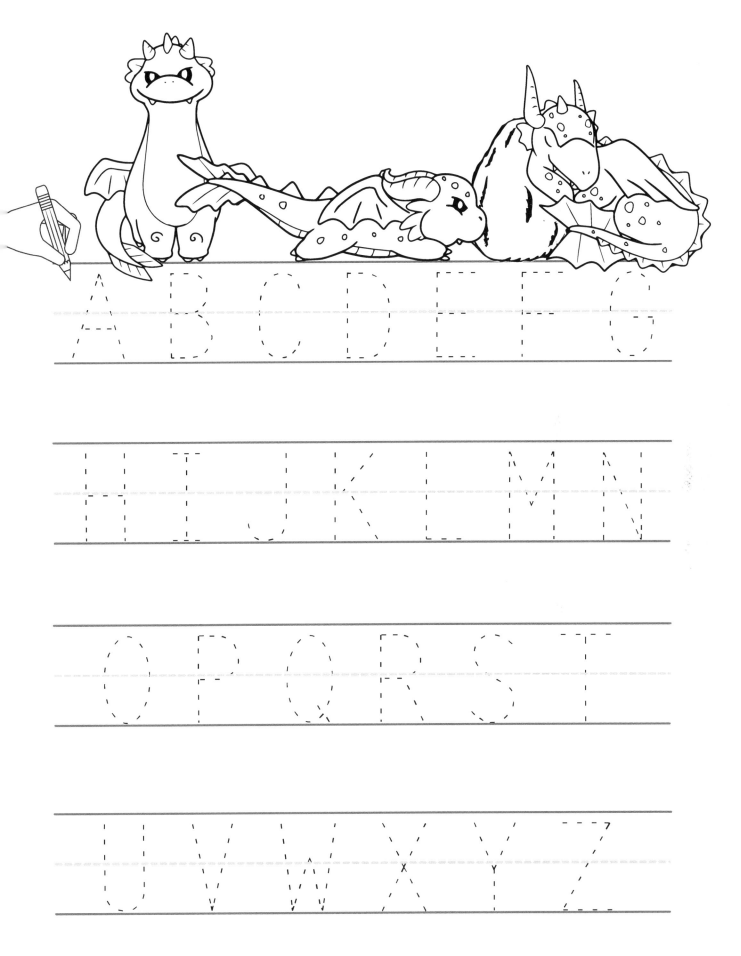

A B C D E F G

H I J K L M N

O P Q R S T

U V W X Y Z

a b c d e f g

h i j k l m n o

p q r s t u v

w x y z

MY FAMILY

Draw a picture of your family and label them. Be sure to include any pets you have!

MY HOME

Draw a picture of your house from the front. Include trees, pets and all the things you see when you come home.

Draw yourself being amazing.

Definition: A a = Amazing - To be surprisingly wonderful. Stunningly impressive.

I am amazing!

I am amazing!

I am amazing!

I am amazing!

I am amazing!

You try it now...

Practice, practice, practice...

You try it now...

One Step Up: You Write It!

I am amazing!

Sentences

I am amazing...

I am amazing, I believe
in myself completely
no matter what.

Draw yourself being brave.

Definition: Adult read to child: B b = Brave - Ready to face anything life brings your way.
Showing much courage.

I am brave!

I am brave!

I am brave!

I am brave!

I am brave!

You try it now...

Practice, practice, practice...

I am brave!
I am brave!
I am brave!
I am brave!
I am brave!
I am brave!
I am brave!

You try it now...

One Step Up: You Write It!

I am brave!

Sentences

I am brave...

I am brave, I always move past and overcome my fears.

Draw yourself being clever.

Definition: C c = Clever - Quick to understand things. Quick to learn and apply ideas to life.

I am clever!

I am clever!

I am clever!

I am clever!

I am clever!

You try it now...

Practice, practice, practice...

I am clever!
I am clever!
I am clever!
I am clever!
I am clever!
I am clever!

You try it now…

One Step Up: You Write It!

I am clever!

Sentences

I am clever...

I am clever, I always
come up with creative
ideas and implement them.

Draw something delightful.

Definition: D d = Delightful - Causing delight, joy and happiness. A charming person.

I am delightful!

I am delightful!

I am delightful!

I am delightful!

I am delightful!

You try it now...

Practice, practice, practice...

I am delightful!
I am delightful!
I am delightful!
I am delightful!
I am delightful!
I am delightful!
I am delightful!

You try it now...

One Step Up: You Write It!

I am delightful!

Sentences

I am delightful...

I am delightful because
I choose to greet every
day with joy and a smile.

Draw yourself being efficient.

Definition: E e = Efficient – Preventing the wasteful use of time, productive, well organized. Does things in an organized and expedient (quick) manner.

I am efficient!

I am efficient!

I am efficient!

I am efficient!

I am efficient!

You try it now...

Practice, practice, practice...

I am efficient!
I am efficient!
I am efficient!
I am efficient!
I am efficient!
I am efficient!
I am efficient!

You try it now...

One Step Up: You Write It!

I am efficient!

Sentences

I am efficient...

I am efficient, I stay focused and finish my work quickly and effectively.

Draw yourself being fearless.

Definition: F f = Fearless - Without fear, someone who is not afraid and goes after what they want.

You try it now...

Practice, practice, practice...

I am fearless!

I am fearless!

I am fearless!

I am fearless!

I am fearless!

I am fearless!

I am fearless!

You try it now...

One Step Up: You Write It!

I am fearless!

Sentences

I am fearless...

I am fearless, I keep trying no matter how scary it feels.

Draw someone you are grateful for.

Definition: G g = Grateful - Feeling or showing an appreciation of kindness; thankful. Feels like a heart full of love. ♡

I am grateful!

I am grateful!

I am grateful!

I am grateful!

I am grateful!

You try it now...

Practice, practice, practice...

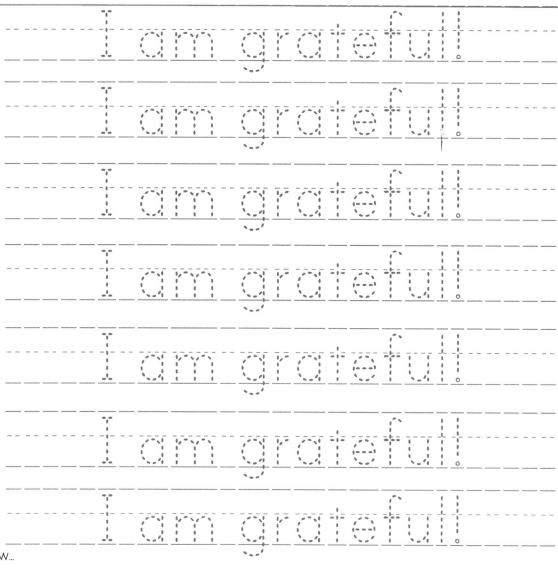

I am grateful!

I am grateful!

I am grateful!

I am grateful!

I am grateful!

I am grateful!

I am grateful!

You try it now...

One Step Up: You Write It!

I am grateful!

Sentences

I am grateful for...

I am grateful for all
the amazing people
I have in my life.

Draw something that makes you happy.

Definition: H h = Happy - Satisfied, content with life. Feeling pleasure and joy in ones heart no matter the circumstances.

I am happy!

I am happy!

I am happy!

I am happy!

I am happy!

You try it now...

Practice, practice, practice...

I am happy!

I am happy!

I am happy!

I am happy!

I am happy!

I am happy!

I am happy!

You try it now...

One Step Up: You Write It!

I am happy!

Sentences

I am happy...

I am happy, I know and
appreciate how blessed
and abundant my life is.

Definition: I i = Intelligent - Having or showing a high level of intelligence.

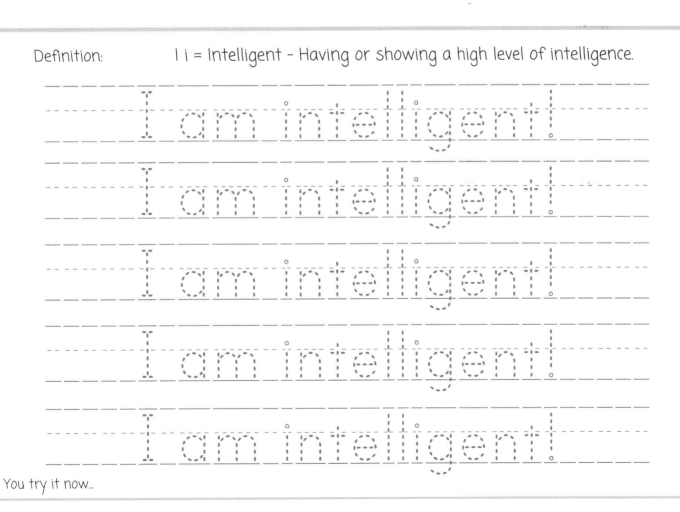

You try it now...

Practice, practice, practice...

I am intelligent!

I am intelligent!

I am intelligent!

I am intelligent!

I am intelligent!

I am intelligent!

I am intelligent!

You try it now...

One Step Up: You Write It!

I am intelligent!

Sentences

I am intelligent...

I am intelligent, I easily find solutions to any challenge.

Draw yourself in a jovial mood.

Definition: J j = Jovial – A cheerful and friendly mood.

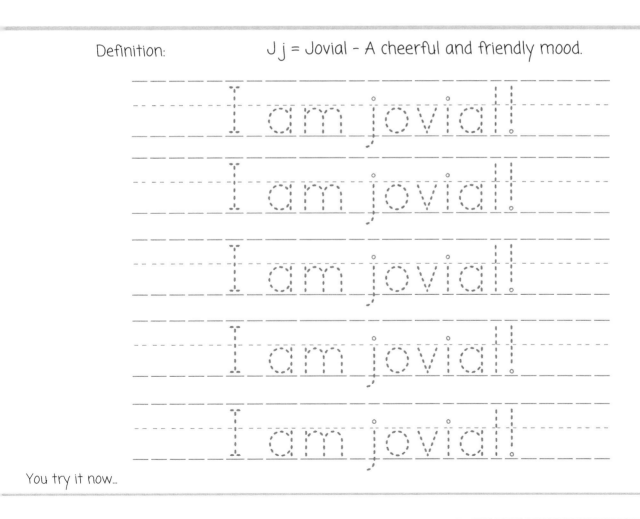

You try it now...

Practice, practice, practice...

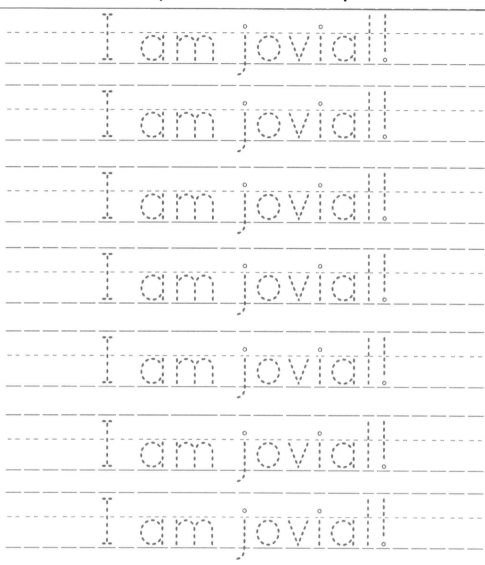

I am jovial!
I am jovial!
I am jovial!
I am jovial!
I am jovial!
I am jovial!
I am jovial!

You try it now...

One Step Up: You Write It!

I am jovial!

Sentences

I am jovial...

I am jovial, I greet life
with a joyful attitude
and an easy smile.

Draw yourself being kind to an animal.

Definition: K k = Kind - Having or showing a friendly, generous and considerate nature.

I am kind!

I am kind!

I am kind!

I am kind!

I am kind!

You try it now...

Practice, practice, practice...

I am kind!

I am kind!

I am kind!

I am kind!

I am kind!

I am kind!

I am kind!

You try it now...

One Step Up: You Write It!

I am kind!

Sentences

I am kind...

I am kind, I care about others and am always willing to help.

Definition: L l = Loved - Showing and or feeling deep affection for on an emotional level.

I am loved!

I am loved!

I am loved!

I am loved!

I am loved!

You try it now...

Practice, practice, practice...

I am loved!

I am loved!

I am loved!

I am loved!

I am loved!

I am loved!

I am loved!

You try it now...

One Step Up: You Write It!

I am loved!

Sentences

I am loved...

I am loved, I know how special I am to everyone who knows me.

Draw something you think is magical.

Definition: M m = Magical - Beautiful and delightful in some extra ordinary way.

I am magical!

I am magical!

I am magical!

I am magical!

I am magical!

You try it now...

Practice, practice, practice...

I am magical!

I am magical!

I am magical!

I am magical!

I am magical!

I am magical!

I am magical!

You try it now...

One Step Up: You Write It!

I am magical!

Sentences

I am magical...

I am magical, I spread
joy and cheer wherever
I go.

Draw someone you think is noble.

N n = Noble - Having or showing high moral qualities, having great character. A good person.

I am noble!

I am noble!

I am noble!

I am noble!

I am noble!

You try it now...

Practice, practice, practice...

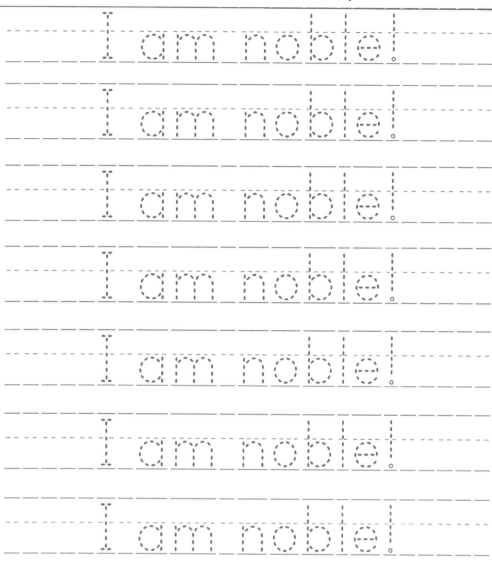

I am noble!

I am noble!

I am noble!

I am noble!

I am noble!

I am noble!

I am noble!

You try it now...

One Step Up: You Write It!

I am noble!

Sentences

I am noble...

I am noble, I treat all others with deep respect and admiration.

What opportunity would you like to have? Draw it.

Definition: O o = Opportunistic – Taking opportunity as it comes. Accepting the challenge of new opportunities with excitement.

I am opportunistic!

I am opportunistic!

I am opportunistic!

I am opportunistic!

I am opportunistic!

You try it now...

Practice, practice, practice...

I am opportunistic!

I am opportunistic!

I am opportunistic!

I am opportunistic!

I am opportunistic!

I am opportunistic!

I am opportunistic!

You try it now...

One Step Up: You Write It!

I am opportunistic!

Sentences

I am opportunistic...

I am opportunistic, I look
for good opportunities
and take them.

Definition: P p = Peaceful - Calm within, restful and at peace emotionally.

I am peaceful!

I am peaceful!

I am peaceful!

I am peaceful!

I am peaceful!

You try it now...

Practice, practice, practice...

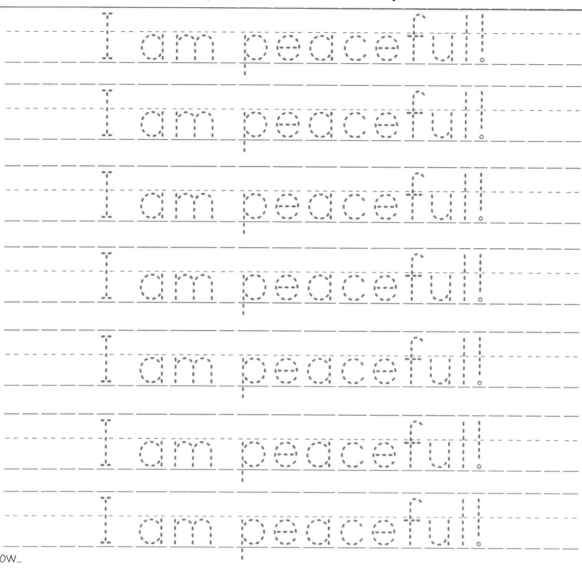

I am peacefull!

I am peacefull!

I am peacefull!

I am peacefull!

I am peacefull!

I am peacefull!

I am peacefull!

You try it now...

One Step Up: You Write It!

I am peaceful!

Sentences

I am peaceful...

I am peaceful, I take
time to quiet my mind
and feel calm within.

Draw something you have questions about.

Definition:

Q q = Questioning - Showing an interest in learning new things. Asking questions in a brave inquisitive way in order to grow ones own knowledge base.

I am questioning!

I am questioning!

I am questioning!

I am questioning!

I am questioning!

You try it now...

Practice, practice, practice...

I am questioning!

I am questioning!

I am questioning!

I am questioning!

I am questioning!

I am questioning!

I am questioning!

You try it now...

One Step Up: You Write It!

I am questioning!

Sentences

I am questioning...

I am questioning, I
love to learn new things
and grow my mind.

Definition: R r = Radiant - Shining, glowing brightly, sending light out into the world.

I am radiant!

I am radiant!

I am radiant!

I am radiant!

I am radiant!

You try it now...

Practice, practice, practice...

I am radiant!

I am radiant!

I am radiant!

I am radiant!

I am radiant!

I am radiant!

I am radiant!

You try it now...

One Step Up: You Write It!

I am radiant!

Sentences

I am radiant...

I am radiant, I
shine everywhere
I go!

Draw something you have had success with.

Definition: S s = Successful - Prosperous, affluent and or wealthy, due to
achievement of ones goals. Achievement.

I am successful!

I am successful!

I am successful!

I am successful!

I am successful!

You try it now...

Practice, practice, practice...

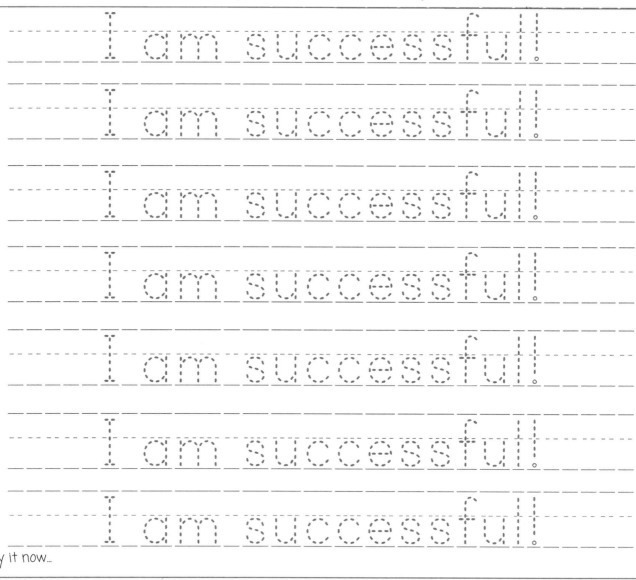

I am successful!

I am successful!

I am successful!

I am successful!

I am successful!

I am successful!

I am successful!

You try it now...

One Step Up: You Write It!

I am successful!

Sentences

I am successful...

I am successful. I
keep trying until
I succeed.

Draw something you would like to transform into.

Definition: T t = Transformable - Able to transform or change at any time.
Change accepted easily. To change form.

I am transformable!

I am transformable!

I am transformable!

I am transformable!

I am transformable!

You try it now...

Practice, practice, practice...

I am transformable!

I am transformable!

I am transformable!

I am transformable!

I am transformable!

I am transformable!

I am transformable!

You try it now...

One Step Up: You Write It!

I am transformable!

Sentences

I am transformable...

I am transformable,

I welcome and appreciate

growth and change.

Draw your unique smile.

Definition: U u = Unique – The only existing one of a kind. – You are the only one that is just like you.
You are unique, we are all unique and amazing in our own ways.

You try it now...

Practice, practice, practice...

I am unique!

I am unique!

I am unique!

I am unique!

I am unique!

I am unique!

I am unique!

You try it now...

One Step Up: You Write It!

I am unique!

Sentences

I am unique...

I am unique, I have
special gifts that no
one else has.

Draw someone or something that is valuable to you.

Definition: V v = Valuable - A thing of great worth, worth a lot, beneficial, of great value.

I am valuable!

I am valuable!

I am valuable!

I am valuable!

I am valuable!

You try it now...

Practice, practice, practice...

I am valuable!

I am valuable!

I am valuable!

I am valuable!

I am valuable!

I am valuable!

I am valuable!

You try it now...

One Step Up: You Write It!

I am valuable!

Sentences

I am valuable...

I am valuable, I know
I am worthy no matter
what others think.

Draw your big worthy heart.

Definition: W w = Worthy - Having enough good qualities to be considered important.
Deserving of respect and praise for such good qualities. Lovable.

I am worthy!

I am worthy!

I am worthy!

I am worthy!

I am worthy!

You try it now...

Practice, practice, practice...

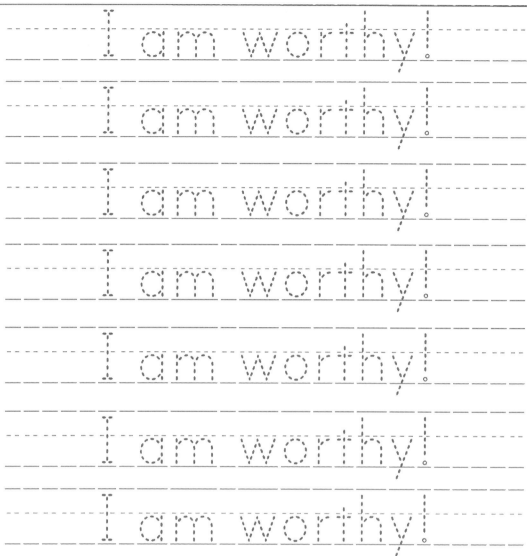

I am worthy!

I am worthy!

I am worthy!

I am worthy!

I am worthy!

I am worthy!

I am worthy!

You try it now...

One Step Up: You Write It!

I am worthy!

Sentences

I am worthy...

I am worthy, I know
I am important and will
achieve my dreams.

Definition: X x = Xenial – Hospitable, welcoming of friendship and community. Kind and friendly.

I am xenial!

I am xenial!

I am xenial!

I am xenial!

I am xenial!

You try it now...

Practice, practice, practice...

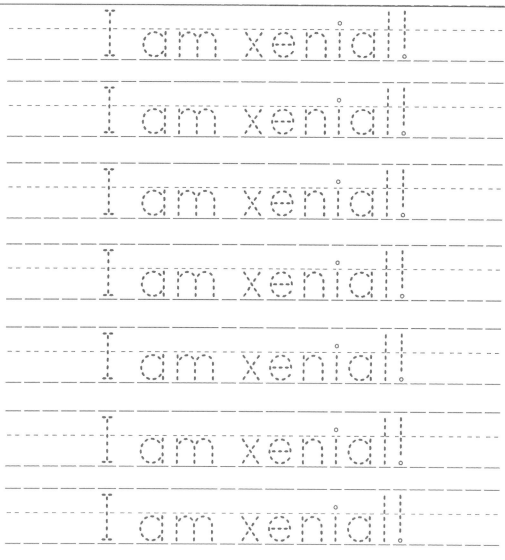

I am xenial!
I am xenial!
I am xenial!
I am xenial!
I am xenial!
I am xenial!
I am xenial!

You try it now...

One Step Up: You Write It!

I am xenial!

Sentences

I am xenial...

I am xenial, I love
being kind, friendly
and helping others.

Definition: Y y = Youthful - Young at heart no matter the age.
Content and glowing in life, remembering to take time to play no matter your age.

I am youthful!

I am youthful!

I am youthful!

I am youthful!

I am youthful!

You try it now...

Practice, practice, practice...

I am youthful!

I am youthful!

I am youthful!

I am youthful!

I am youthful!

I am youthful!

I am youthful!

You try it now...

One Step Up: You Write It!

I am youthful!

Sentences

I am youthful...

I am youthful, I always
remember to play, laugh
and have fun.

Draw yourself dancing and full of energy. Zestfully.

Definition: Z z = Zestful – Full of energy, ready to take on anything. Full of life and the joy of it.

I am zestful!

I am zestful!

I am zestful!

I am zestful!

I am zestful!

You try it now...

Practice, practice, practice...

I am zestful!
I am zestful!
I am zestful!
I am zestful!
I am zestful!
I am zestful!
I am zestful!

You try it now...

One Step Up: You Write It!

I am zestful!

Sentences

I am zestful...

I am zestful, I love to
live my life to the fullest
with joy in my heart.

How do positive affirmations work?

Science has proven that positive affirmations help us to build a positive self view. When we practice repeating and feeling the affirmations to be true, this gives us a mindset that allows for us to meet and greet challenges with a very solution oriented process of thought because we believe that we can handle anything that comes our way. We believe in our capability to handle all challenges. Even the ones that would stop others who do not practice positive self affirming in their tracks.

When we believe that we can handle anything that comes our way, we are able to embrace challenges instead of avoiding them or being overwhelmed by them. When we become overwhelmed, it then becomes easy to slip into a poor state of mental health.

Positive affirmations when used regularly help to build our self love and personal empowerment.

If we can provide these uplifting ways of thinking about oneself to our children and in ourselves, we can begin to help create a ripple effect throughout the human race. If we teach our kids these tools young and they implement them throughout their lives, not only will they be more successful and able to handle hard challenges with ease. They will then teach their kids and their kids will teach their kids and so on. We parent how our parents parent in so many ways. If we as adults teach our own children these success tools now, they WILL carry it into their adulthood and they will raise more resilient kids as well.

We are truly on the forefront of parenting here. We are, in using these tools, shaping generations to come.

One note I have to mention is that it is essential that you model the behavior you WANT for your kids. If you want them to be happy and healthy, you must find a way to create that within yourself. We are not perfect and we may not always be present enough to practice mindfulness all the time but when we do become present, it is a great time to do success practices for yourself and with your kids.

Positive affirmations are not the only tool to high level mental wellbeing and a success mindset, it takes a toolbox and they don't work unless they are practiced and repeated consistently. They are not going to change any situation that comes up, the change is in how you and your kids are able to navigate anything that may arise.

Now, help change the generations of the world. We are the leaders, let's lead.

Made in the USA
Columbia, SC
27 March 2025

55738306R00070